...tainer,
...er.'

...an remember Trevor when he started out as an excited
...d enthusiastic stylist. It was clear to me even then
...at he would make a lasting impact on the world of
...airdressing and he has fulfilled my expectations. He
...ontinues to remain fresh and energetic and never fails to
...ommunicate his passion for our art. Well done Trevor!'

Annie Humphreys

'I have always admir... ...hair and love of
hairdressing. It has without doubt made him one of the most
respected hair artists in the world today. His dedication to his
work within the industry, his TV appearances and media attention,
have helped win the hairdressing profession the respectability it
deserves. Long may Trevor continue.'

Robert Lobetta

'Trevor is one of the very few truly influential members of our craft. A great
talent, a great professional, and one of the nicest people in the business.'

'Trevor has been the biggest influence in my career,
and the knowledge that I have gained working
alongside him has given me the strength to express
myself in a creative way. I shall always have
special memories of Trevor.'

Antoinette Beenders.

'Trevor is amazingly talented, and his passion
and enthusiasm are a total inspiration.'

Michael Gordon   Bumble + bumble
New York

The person who follows the crowd will usually go no further
than the crowd. The person who walks along will find
themselves in places that no-one has ever been before.
So it is with creativity.
So it is with Trevor Sorbie.

Vivienne Mackinder

'Here is a person that is an industry legend. He has affected
my life and countless others positively with inspirational
work and words. Trevor's influence on our industry could never
be summed up in a few words. Here are but a few that are on
hairdressers' lips world-wide, as they are on mine: Mentor,
inspirational, creative genius, humble and giving.'

Chris Baran

'Trevor believed in me. If it wasn't for
him, I wouldn't be where I am today. It is
more than an honour to have worked with
him and an honour to know him.'

Ruth Roche

'Trevor is amazing to me in his ability to re-invent himself in his
art. He never ceases to go beyond, yet always with beauty and a
style of his own. He has shown years of dedication to our industry
with his teaching and show work, yet remains humble and
personable. Trevor is definit... ...to look up to.'

...ue to himself and his
...with a great heart,
...umour. His
...s to our...

'Here is a person that i...
has affected my life an...
positively with inspir...
...luence on...

trevor sorbie
VISIONS IN HAIR

Compiled and written by
Kris Sorbie and Jacki Wadeson

© Trevor Sorbie and Jacki Wadeson 1998

First published 1998 by
MACMILLAN PRESS LTD
Houndmills, Basingstoke, Hampshire RG21 6XS
and London
Companies and representatives
throughout the world

ISBN 0–333–74714–3

A catalogue record for this book is available from the British Library.

This book is printed on paper suitable for recycling and made from fully managed and sustained forest sources.

10   9   8   7   6   5   4   3   2   1
07   06   05   04   03   02   01   00   99   98

Printed in Great Britain by Jarrold Book Printing, Thetford, Norfolk

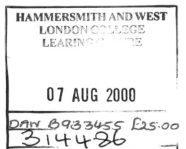

CONTENTS

TO MY WIFE, KRIS, WITHOUT WHOSE HELP AND SUPPORT I COULD NEVER HAVE ACHIEVED WHAT I HAVE IN THE WORLD OF HAIRDRESSING. WITHOUT HER, THIS BOOK WOULD NOT HAVE BEEN POSSIBLE.

TREVOR SORBIE

INTRODUCTION

THE SHOWMAN OF ALL HAIRDRESSERS, TREVOR SORBIE IS
ADMIRED BY THE HAIRDRESSING INDUSTRY WORLDWIDE.
FUNNY, CHARMING AND ELOQUENT, HE IS A MAN OF VISION
WHO IS TRULY ONE OF THE WORLD'S GREATEST ARTISTS.

AHEAD OF HIS TIME, TREVOR SORBIE CONTINUES TO CHANGE
THE FACE OF THE INTERNATIONAL HAIRDRESSING SCENE. HIS
INCREDIBLE ARTISTRY HAS BEEN INSTRUMENTAL IN ELEVATING
HAIRDRESSING TO AN ART FORM. HIS PIONEERING TECHNIQUES
AND CUTS – THE WEDGE, THE CHOP, THE SCRUNCH – ARE
NOW PART OF EVERYDAY SALON PARLANCE. WHEN HE CREATES
A NEW LOOK, HE MAKES EVERY HAIRDRESSER SIMPLY WISH
THEY HAD THOUGHT OF IT FIRST.

NO OTHER HAIRDRESSER IS SO FINELY TUNED TO THE NEED
ALWAYS TO BE ONE STEP AHEAD, TO BREAK DOWN BARRIERS,
TO BE AT THE CUTTING EDGE. HIS HAIRDRESSING IS VISIONARY,
HIS SHOWS ARE SPELLBINDING, AND HIS ABILITY TO WIN EVERY
TOP AWARD IS COVETED BY HIS PEERS. DRIVEN BY ARTISTIC
ENERGY, HE THINKS LATERALLY, TAKES THE OBVIOUS, AND WITH
A SIMPLE TWIST, CREATES A NEW CONCEPT THAT LEAVES AN
INDELIBLE MARK ON THE WORLD OF HAIR. THIS BOOK IS A
PICTORIAL INSIGHT INTO IMAGES THAT TRACE THE LIFE AND
WORK OF THE MAN WHO HAS BECOME A LEGEND IN HIS
OWN LIFETIME.

JACKI WADESON

profile

1949 ... Born Paisley, Scotland

1959 ... Paisley School of Art, Scotland

1964 ... Apprentice barber to father, Ilford

1969 ... Opened a barbershop, Edmonton

1970 ... Richard Henry School of Hairdressing

1970 ... Stylist at Henri, Loughton

1971 ... Stylist at Selfridges, Ilford

1972 ... Stylist at Vidal Sassoon

1973 ... Artistic Director, Vidal Sassoon

1978 ... Stylist and session hairdresser at
         Toni & Guy and then John Frieda

1979 ... Opened Trevor Sorbie salon,
         Covent Garden, London

1985 ... **British** Hairdresser of the Year

1986 ... Created the Trevor Sorbie Professional
         product line

1986 ... **British** Hairdresser of the year

1991 ... **British** Hairdresser of the Year

1992 ... **British** Hairdresser of the Year

THE EARLY YEARS

THE

PATRICK HUNT

WEDGE

1974

I WAS NEVER CUT OUT TO BE AN ACADEMIC – MY BEST
SUBJECTS AT SCHOOL WERE ART AND SPORT. I DREAMT OF
BECOMING AN ARTIST BUT MY SCHOOLDAYS ENDED ABRUPTLY
WHEN I LEFT SCHOOL AT THE AGE OF 15. THE FACTORY FLOOR
BECKONED UNTIL MY FATHER SUGGESTED THAT I SHOULD HELP
OUT IN HIS BARBERSHOP. SHAMPOOING AND SWEEPING UP
WERE THE ORDER OF THE DAY UNTIL, THREE MONTHS LATER,
SOMETHING HAPPENED THAT WAS TO CHANGE MY LIFE.

A REGULAR CLIENT SAID, RATHER RASHLY, 'COME ON TREVOR,
ISN'T IT ABOUT TIME YOU DID A HAIRCUT?' AS I WIELDED THE
CLIPPERS TO GIVE HIM A NO. 2, I FOUND I LOVED THE SENSATION
OF CUTTING HAIR AND I DIDN'T FIND IT DIFFICULT. IT CREATED AN
EXCITEMENT WITHIN ME THAT LIVES ON TO THIS DAY.

AFTER FIVE YEARS OF BARBERING, I WAS GETTING BORED AND
NEEDED A NEW CHALLENGE. THE OBVIOUS PROGRESSION WAS
TO VENTURE INTO THE WORLD OF LADIES' HAIRDRESSING. MY
PARENTS PAID FOR ME TO GO TO THE RICHARD HENRY SCHOOL.
THE PRINCIPAL SAW IN ME A TALENT THAT I WASN'T EVEN AWARE
OF. HE SUGGESTED I GO TO A 'GOOD HOUSE', MEANING A TOP
SALON. AT THAT TIME, I DIDN'T FEEL I HAD THE CONFIDENCE TO
WORK IN THE WEST END, SO I DECIDED TO LEARN MY ART IN A
LESS INTIMIDATING ENVIRONMENT IN ESSEX.

BY THE LATE 70s, LONDON'S FASHION SCENE WAS EXPLODING.
SASSOON HAD REVOLUTIONISED WOMEN'S HAIRDRESSING BY
RE-INVENTING THE BOB. BEFORE THAT, HAIR HAD BEEN WORN
UP, EITHER IN BOUFFANTS OR BEEHIVES, BUT THE LOOSE FLAT
HAIR OF THE SASSOON ERA SIGNALLED A NEW BEGINNING. I
JOINED SASSOON'S, AND MY BIG BREAK CAME WHEN I CREATED
A HAIRCUT WHICH I CALLED THE WEDGE. THIS WAS THE FIRST
HAIRDRESSING PICTURE TO BE PUBLISHED AS A DOUBLE-PAGE
SPREAD IN *VOGUE* MAGAZINE. SEEING MY WORK IN PRINT WAS
INSPIRATIONAL. THE WEDGE CAPTURED THE SPIRIT OF THE TIME
AND WAS FLAUNTED IN NIGHTCLUBS AROUND THE WORLD. I
NOW UNDERSTOOD THE POWER OF INVENTION. IF I COULD
ACHIEVE THIS ONCE, THEN SURELY I COULD DO IT AGAIN...

MY VERY FIRST HAIR PICTURE UNDER MY OWN
NAME. IT WAS TAKEN AT A SHOW IN
SWITZERLAND, WHEN I RECEIVED MY FIRST
STANDING OVATION –
I LOVED THE HIGH THAT IT GAVE ME.

A FUTURISTIC IMAGE CREATED FOR AN ADVERTISEMENT WITH TOP PHOTOGRAPHER JOHN SWANNELL. MY BRIEF WAS TO EPITOMISE THE YEAR 2000.

I LOVE SIMPLE THINGS – THIS HAIRCUT IS CHARACTERISED BY PURITY OF LINE AND HAS A TIMELESS QUALITY.

IN MY EARLY YEARS I WAS
VERY EXPERIMENTAL AND THIS
IS AN EXAMPLE OF THE KIND
OF SHAPES I WAS CARVING
INTO HAIR AT THE TIME.

1979

DURING THIS PERIOD, I WAS A STYLIST AT THE JOHN FRIEDA SALON. HIS METHOD OF FINISHING AT THAT TIME WAS FINGER-DRYING. IT WAS A GREAT TECHNIQUE BUT TOOK AGES.

ONE DAY I WAS EXTREMELY BUSY; I HAD THREE CLIENTS WAITING, AND WAS UNDER A GREAT DEAL OF PRESSURE. MY NEXT CLIENT HAD THICK, RED, POROUS, WAVY HAIR AND, OF COURSE, SHE WANTED IT FINGER-DRIED. BECAUSE OF THE BACKLOG OF CLIENTS, I ASKED HER IF I COULD SPEED UP THE PROCESS BY ADDING HEAT.

I FOUND THAT BY TAKING A HANDFUL OF HAIR, SQUEEZING IT IN MY HAND AND APPLYING HEAT, THEN ALLOWING THE HAIR TO COOL I COULD CREATE VOLUME. I REALISED THAT I HAD INADVERTENTLY DISCOVERED A NEW METHOD OF DRYING. I EXPERIMENTED USING THIS TECHNIQUE ON ALL TYPES AND LENGTHS OF HAIR. EACH TIME, EVEN ON THE FINEST HAIR, I ACHIEVED INCREDIBLE RESULTS, ADDING VOLUME AND TEXTURE I'D NEVER SEEN BEFORE. THUS, SCRUNCH DRYING, PERHAPS MY GREATEST INVENTION, WAS BORN...

THE **SCRUNCH**

1980

PUNK WAS A GENERATION OF YOUNG PEOPLE WHO WERE ANTI-ESTABLISHMENT. THEIR HAIR WAS AN AGGRESSIVE STATEMENT OF THEIR FEELINGS. IT WAS A GLORIOUS CELEBRATION OF YOUTH AND IT INSPIRED ME BECAUSE IT WAS THE OPPOSITE OF EVERYTHING THAT WAS HAPPENING AT THE TIME.

I TOOK MY INSPIRATION FROM THE STREETS AND TURNED IT AROUND. INSTEAD OF ALLOWING HAIR TO LIE FLAT, I MADE IT STAND OUT. INSTEAD OF BLUNT CUTTING, I RAZOR CUT TO CREATE TEXTURE. INSTEAD OF APPLYING COLOUR ALL OVER, I APPLIED IT TO JUST THE ENDS. IT WAS AN EXPERIMENT, COMBINING ALL THESE TECHNIQUES, THAT CREATED THE WOLFMAN, WHICH I PRESENTED AT THE WORLD HAIRDRESSING CONGRESS SHOW AT THE ROYAL ALBERT HALL IN LONDON.

THE **WOLFMAN**

1981

USING THE SAME PHILOSOPHY AS WHEN I CREATED THE WOLFMAN, I TRIED DESIGNING SOMETHING THAT WAS REALLY NEW. SURELY, THE OPPOSITE OF A GOOD HAIRCUT WOULD BE A BAD HAIRCUT BUT NOT IN THE SENSE OF BAD TASTE.

I USED THE BASIS OF A BOB AS THE OUTLINE SHAPE BUT REDEFINED THE INTERIOR. I WAS HOLDING SECTIONS AS NORMAL, BUT, INSTEAD OF CUTTING THE ENDS OF THE HAIR, I CUT INTO THE LENGTHS AT RANDOM. WITH A MENTAL VISION OF WHAT I WANTED, I USED INTUITION AS MY TECHNIQUE. I FOLLOWED MY GUT FEELING AND GAVE THE CLASSIC BOB A NEW TEXTURE.

THIS NEW METHOD CREATED TEXTURISING, A TECHNIQUE WHICH HAD NEVER BEEN USED BEFORE. IT WAS SOON TO BECOME PART OF EVERY HAIRDRESSER'S REPERTOIRE. BASICALLY, IT WAS A CONTINUATION OF THE CONCEPT BEHIND THE WOLFMAN, TAKING THE OPPOSITE OF WHAT WAS THE NORM, AND WORKING FROM THE HEART, AS OPPOSED TO USING PRECISION CUTTING TECHNIQUES. IT WAS A BRAVE MOVE THAT STARTED A REVOLUTION IN HAIR CUTTING, OPENING THE DOOR TO TEXTURED HAIRCUTS, WHICH HAVE DEVELOPED INTO TODAY'S TOTALLY FREEHAND TECHNIQUES.

THE **CHOP**

MY
INSPIRATION
AND
MOTIVATION

'The future of anything is in forward progression.'

TO MANY PEOPLE'S EXASPERATION, I HAVE ALWAYS BEEN A REBEL. I AM RELENTLESS IN MY QUEST TO ACHIEVE AND CREATE HAIRSTYLES THAT MAKE HAIRDRESSERS SIT UP AND TAKE NOTICE. THIS IS A VERY SELF-INDULGENT PART OF MY NATURE.

I HAVE NEVER BEEN CONTENT IN KNOWING WHAT I KNOW; I AM MORE INTERESTED IN WHAT I DON'T KNOW. THIS ATTITUDE KEEPS ME DISCIPLINED IN MY BASIC SKILLS AND STIMULATES ME TO CREATE NEW IDEAS. I DON'T RESTRICT MYSELF BY STAYING WITHIN THE BOUNDARIES OF HAIRDRESSING. I LOOK AT OTHER MEDIA – ART, ARCHITECTURE, NATURE, SCULPTURE – AND ATTITUDES OF THE MOMENT AND BREAK BOUNDARIES BY APPLYING THIS KNOWLEDGE TO THE FABRIC OF HAIR.

FEATHER

'The inspiration behind a hairstyle can be as simple as an everyday object.'

HAIRCLIP

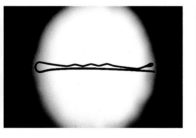

'Ideas are all around us – all we have to do is look beyond the obvious.'

IRON GATE

SPIDER PLANT

**'Doing what I do is easy;
thinking of what I do is
difficult.'**

ALISTAIR HUGHES

PETROL STATION SIGN

BRANCHES

ALISTAIR HUGHES

23

'The simplest and strongest shapes are those of the geometrics.'

PLAYING CARD

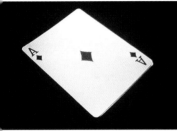

CHESS-BOARD

'Nature provides us with textures, colours and shapes that can be translated onto hair.'

PLUMES

PINEAPPLE

'Be bold, be different, but always do everything in good taste.'

PIECE OF FUR

PENGUIN

THE
COLLECTIONS

THE DESERT SHOOT

THIS PHOTOGRAPHIC SHOOT WAS AN EXAMPLE OF APPLYING MY PHILOSOPHY OF ALWAYS DOING THE OPPOSITE OF WHAT IS EXPECTED.

I DECIDED TO TAKE FASHION OUT OF CONTEXT – TO SHOOT GLAMOUR AGAINST THE BACKDROP OF THE WILDERNESS OF A DESERT. I WANTED TO PUSH AWAY BARRIERS AND DO SOMETHING THAT HAD NEVER BEEN DONE BEFORE.

CONDITIONS WERE DIFFICULT. IT WAS HOT AND DUSTY AND WE COULD ONLY SHOOT IN THE VERY EARLY MORNING OR LATE EVENING. THE RESULTS WERE WORTH IT. THEY SHOW THE FRAGILITY OF GLAMOUR AGAINST THE FORCE OF NATURE.

A LIZARD-LIKE POSE CAPTURES
THE ECLECTIC COMBINATION OF
NATURE AND GLAMOUR.

A STRATEGICALLY PLACED
WIND MACHINE BEHIND THE
MODEL ENABLED US TO DEFY
THE LAW OF GRAVITY.

I LOVE THIS PICTURE BECAUSE
IT IS SO HARD AND SIMPLE,
WITH AN INCREDIBLE INTENSITY
OF COLOUR.

THE TEXTURE OF THE CACTUS
IS MIRRORED IN THE HAIR.

35

SHADOW
PLAY

THE SECRET OF THIS COLLECTION'S STRENGTH
IS ITS SIMPLICITY.

THIS IS ONE OF MY FAVOURITE SETS OF PICTURES. THE
PHOTOGRAPHER'S IDEA OF SHAKING THE CAMERA WHILE
TAKING THE SHOT CREATED THE SOFT EDGE ON ONE SIDE.
EXAGGERATED SHAPES AND SHADOWY LIGHTING GIVE A
SURREAL FEEL TO THE IMAGES AND PORTRAY A
PROFOUND BEAUTY.

I'VE TAKEN ONE PART OF EACH
STYLE AND EXAGGERATED IT TO
ACCENTUATE THE SHAPES.

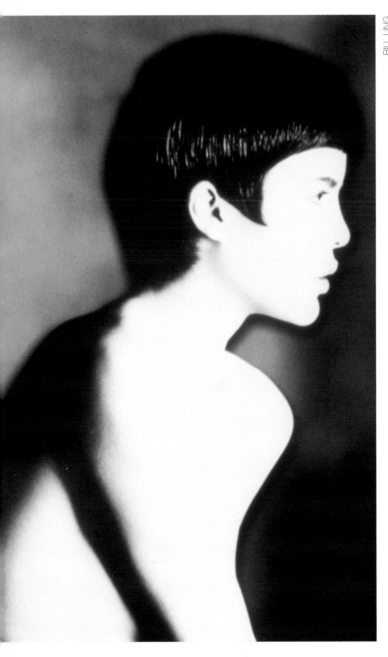

I LOVE THE ANDROGYNOUS
QUALITY.

IT'S TIMELESS – 50 YEARS FROM
NOW THIS IMAGE WILL STILL
WORK.

THE PERFECT EXAMPLE OF THE
WAY A MODEL CAN TRANSLATE
A LOOK INTO A MOOD.

PRIMARY
COLOURS

WHEN I ASK OTHER HAIRDRESSERS WHAT MAKES A GOOD HAIR
PICTURE, THE ANSWER IS, INVARIABLY, THE HAIR. I DISAGREE. I
FEEL IT STARTS WITH THE RIGHT FACE, THEN BY THE USE OF
WIGS OR HAIRPIECES A LOOK IS CREATED THAT FORMS A
HARMONIOUS RELATIONSHIP BETWEEN FACE AND HAIR.

THIS COLLECTION OF PHOTOGRAPHS IS A GOOD EXAMPLE OF
HOW I'VE CHOSEN MODELS PURELY FOR THEIR FACES AND
USED WIGS TO CREATE THE LOOKS. THESE IMAGES WON ME
THE BRITISH HAIRDRESSER OF THE YEAR AWARD 1991.

WOULD YOU BELIEVE THIS
MODEL HAS SHOULDER-
LENGTH BROWN HAIR.

41

DIFFERENT POSES HELP TO
ENCAPSULATE FEELING AND
ADD A SENSE OF HUMOUR TO
PHOTOGRAPHS.

42

BOTH THESE GIRLS' OWN
NATURAL HAIR IS DARK AND
SHOULDER LENGTH. SEE HOW,
WITH THE CLEVER CUSTOMISING
OF A WIG, WE CAN COMPLETELY
TRANSFORM THEIR LOOKS.

43

THE STARCK COLLECTION

PHILIPPE STARCK IS PROBABLY THE MOST INFLUENTIAL ARCHITECT/DESIGNER IN THE WORLD. I WAS FIRST INTRODUCED TO HIS WORK WHEN I STAYED AT THE PARAMOUNT HOTEL IN NEW YORK. HE USES SIMPLICITY AS A BASE, ADDS A TWIST, AND THE WORK IS TRANSFORMED INTO ART.

IN THIS COLLECTION I USED HIS FURNITURE AS A PROP, AND WE SHOT THE ENTIRE COLLECTION ON A PLATE CAMERA. THIS TYPE OF PHOTOGRAPHY GIVES A QUALITY THAT SURPASSES ALL OTHERS. THE HAIR REFLECTS DIFFERENT DECADES FROM THE 30s TO THE 90s.

A HARMONIOUS COMPOSITION
WHERE ALL THE ELEMENTS
WORK TOGETHER.

THE SPIKE LEG OF THE CHAIR
INSPIRED THE HAIRSTYLE.

46

THIS WAS MY TRANSLATION OF
THE 70s REVIVAL.

SHORT AND SPIKY – SO DIFFERENT FROM
THIS MODEL'S IMAGE AS A BLONDE ON
p. 43. ANOTHER ILLUSTRATION OF THE
FLEXIBILITY OF WIGS.

ONE OF MY FIRST ATTEMPTS TO
GET AWAY FROM THE STANDARD
HEAD AND SHOULDERS PICTURE.

49

FLOWER POWER

ONE OF MY FAVOURITE PHOTOGRAPHERS IS MARK HAVRILIAK, WHO LIVES IN NEW YORK. ONE DAY HE SUGGESTED THE IDEA OF MODELS SURROUNDED BY FLOWERS. THE CONCEPT DIDN'T APPEAL TO ME UNTIL MARK CONVINCED ME BY DOING A TEST TO ILLUSTRATE HIS IDEA.

ON THE SHOOT, IT TOOK MORE TIME TO ARRANGE THE FLOWERS THAN IT DID TO DO THE HAIR AND MAKE-UP, BUT I LOVED THE LOOK AND FEEL IN THE PICTURES. INTERESTINGLY ENOUGH, TO THIS DAY, WHEN PEOPLE LOOK AT MARK'S PORTFOLIO, THEY STILL SAY THAT THESE ARE THE MOST STUNNING IMAGES THAT HE HAS EVER CREATED FOR A HAIRDRESSER.

MARK HAVRILIAK

A STRIKING BLEND OF VIVID COLOURS PORTRAYS A POWERFUL IMAGE.

TINY, SNAKE-LIKE PIECES OF HAIR
WERE ADDED TO NATURAL CURL
TO GIVE THIS AN INDIVIDUAL,
SEPARATED TEXTURE.

THE ORIGINAL BARBIE DOLL!

MY MODEL'S HIGHLIGHTS HAD
GROWN OUT, LEAVING A REGROWTH
THAT PERFECTLY COMPLEMENTED
THE LOOK I WANTED.

MIRROR
IMAGE

A PHOTOGRAPHER AND A HAIRDRESSER HAVE TO BE IN TUNE. THEY NEED TO BE ON THE SAME WAVELENGTH IN ORDER TO ACHIEVE SUCCESS.

THE NEXT THREE PICTURES ARE EXAMPLES OF THE PHOTOGRAPHER TAKING IMAGERY ONE STEP BEYOND THE ORIGINAL CONCEPT. AFTER THE SHOOT, MARK HAVRILIAK FELT THE PICTURES HADN'T REACHED THEIR FULL POTENTIAL, SO HE SET ABOUT HAND-COLOURING AND DISTORTING SOME OF THE OUT-TAKES. THE RESULT JUST GOES TO SHOW HOW IMPORTANT IT IS TO WORK WITH SOMEONE WHO IS NEVER CONTENT TO DO JUST WHAT IS NECESSARY BUT WHO PUSHES BOTH HIS OWN AND YOUR CREATIVE ABILITY TO THE LIMIT.

56

NEW YORK
NEW YORK

THIS METROPOLIS, THE PULSE OF AMERICA, EXCITES AND STIMULATES ME. I TRY TO SHOOT THERE AS OFTEN AS I CAN BECAUSE OF THE ENERGY THE CITY EXUDES.

THESE PICTURES ENCAPSULATE STREET CRED – THEY COMBINE RAWNESS WITH A HARD EDGE AND ARE A VISION OF TODAY'S YOUTH. IN ORDER TO GET THE RIGHT FEELING INTO THE SHOTS, WE HAD TO PHOTOGRAPH IN SOME OF THE TOUGHEST PARTS – HARLEM, THE BOWERY AND THE SUBWAYS. WE EVEN HAD AN ARMED BODYGUARD. I NEEDED TO FEEL THAT ELEMENT OF DANGER, WHICH I HOPED WOULD TRANSLATE INTO THE MOOD OF THE PICTURES.

60

SIMPLE
LINES

PONYTAILS WERE MY INSPIRATION FOR THIS SHOOT. NOTICE
THE DIFFERENT TEXTURES – THE HAIR IS SCULPTED LIKE REEDS,
CURLS LIKE SNAKES, WAVES INTO TENDRILS AND SPLAYS LIKE
A HORSE'S TAIL.

THE IMAGES WERE OFFSET AGAINST WHITE SPACE TO PLAY ON
THE PURITY OF LINE AND BRING A NEW DIMENSION TO THIS
COLLECTION. WE SHOT IN BLACK AND WHITE AND HAND-
COLOURED THE PRINTS, ADDING A WASH OF COLOUR TO GIVE
YET ANOTHER DIMENSION TO THE PICTURE.

STREET
WISE

HERE I EXPERIMENTED USING A DIFFERENT PHOTOGRAPHER, DAVID WOOLLEY. I HAD SEEN HIS WORK AND ARRANGED A MEETING TO SEE IF WE FELT WE WERE ON THE SAME WAVELENGTH. AFTER WE MET I WAS CONVINCED THAT HE NOT ONLY UNDERSTOOD ME BUT COULD ALSO HELP ME DEVELOP MY IDEAS.

IN THIS COLLECTION DAVID USED A WIDE-ANGLE LENS TO GIVE A SLIGHT DISTORTION TO THE IMAGES. I LOVED THE AWKWARDNESS OF THE GIRLS' POSES – THE PICTURES ENCAPSULATED AN EDITORIAL FREEDOM THAT WAS FRESH AND INSPIRING.

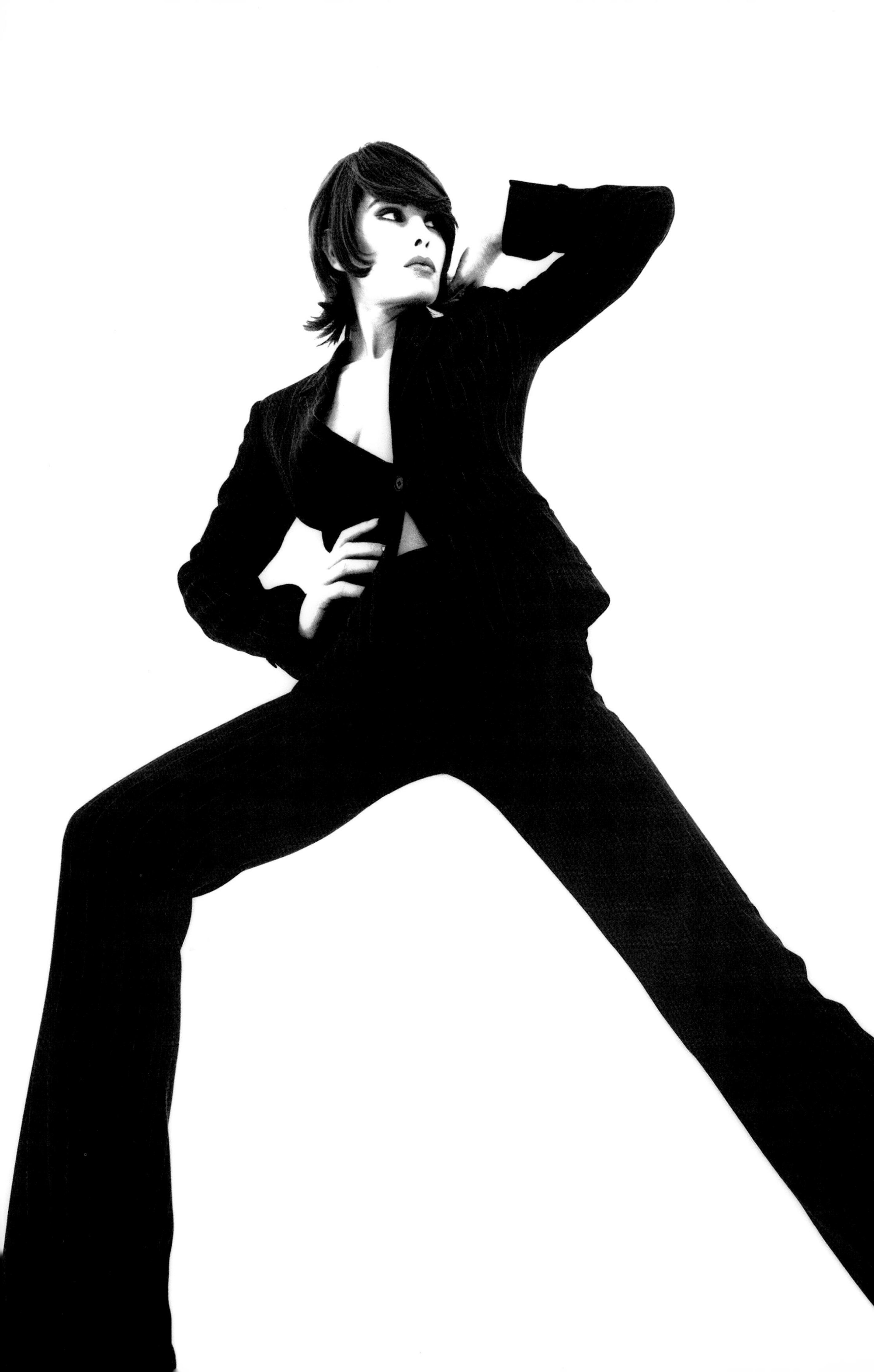

DAVID WOOLLEY

THE POP GROUP OASIS WAS
THE INSPIRATION FOR THIS
IMAGE, NOT ONLY IN STYLE BUT
ALSO IN THE ATTITUDE.

MAKING HAIR LOOK 'UNDONE' IS
MORE OF AN ART THAN IT
LOOKS.

NOT A VERY LADYLIKE POSE
BUT IT WORKS FOR ME.

INSPIRED BY THE MOHICAN,
THIS SHORT CUT IS BOTH
FEMININE AND FUNKY.

71

THE MODEL'S QUIRKY EXPRESSION IS REFLECTED IN THE SHAPE OF THE HAIR.

BY INTERLOCKING RINGLETS, I CREATED THESE COILS WHICH PRODUCED A MODERN WAY OF WEARING LONG HAIR.

WHITE
MISCHIEF

FOR THIS COLLECTION WITH DAVID WOOLLEY, I TRIED TO GET A
TRIBAL FEEL INTO THE HAIR AND STYLING. I STUDIED
HEADDRESSES AND USED HAIRPIECES IN DIFFERENT COLOURS
TO GIVE TEXTURE AND DEFINITION. I WANTED TO MAKE THE HAIR
LOOK TOUCHABLE, NOT SET OR OVERLY CONTRIVED.

FOR ME, ONE OF THE SECRETS OF A GOOD HAIRSTYLE IS NOT
TO MAKE THE LOOK CONSTRUCTED – IT SHOULD HAVE A
FREEDOM AND AN EMPATHY WITH NATURE.

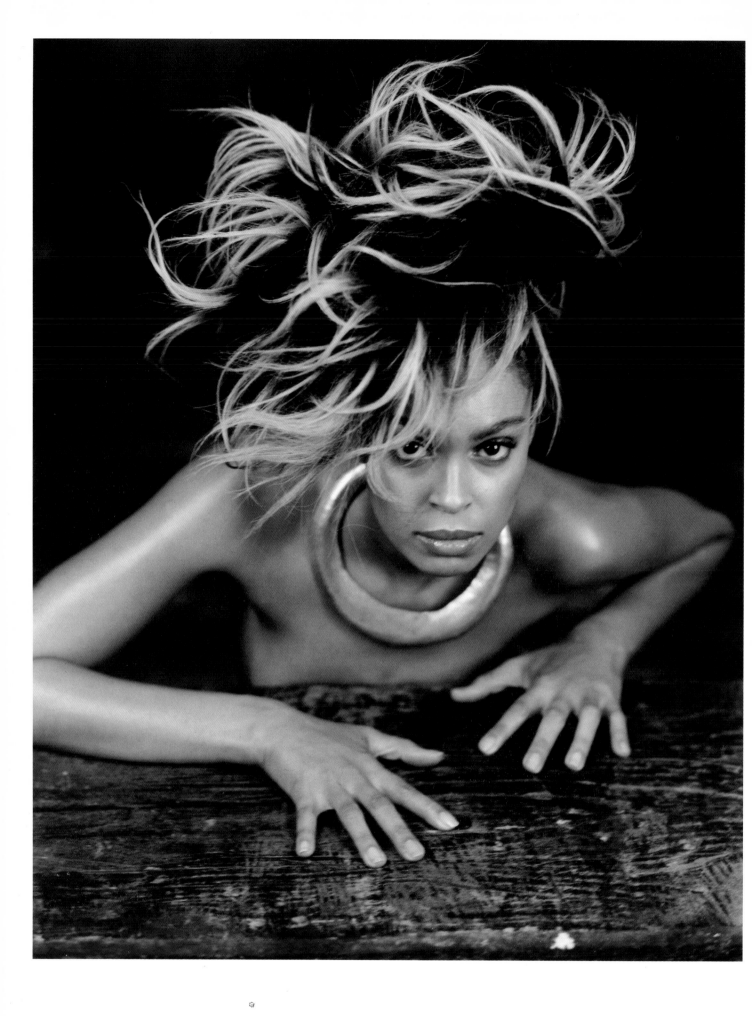

HAIR HAS A CHAMELEON QUALITY.
HERE, THROUGH COLOUR AND
TEXTURE, IT IS TRANSFORMED TO
LOOK LIKE FUR.

THE COLOUR STORY

FOR THIS SESSION WITH MARK HAVRILIAK, WE BRAINSTORMED, POOLING THE CREATIVE ENERGIES OF THE ART TEAM TO COME UP WITH A DIRECTION AND FEEL FOR THE PHOTOGRAPHY.

THE SECRET OF THESE IMAGES WAS THE USE OF WHAT I CONSIDER TO BE A REVOLUTION IN HAIRPIECES – COLOURED WEFTS OF HAIR. CREATED BY MY WIFE, KRIS, THESE ARE COLOURED USING A BLENDING TECHNIQUE THAT GRADUATES FROM DARK BROWN AT THE ROOTS, THROUGH THE VIBRANCY OF RED AND ORANGE, AND FINALLY FADES TO BLONDE. THE ESSENCE IS THAT THERE ARE NO DEFINING LINES. SMALL WIG COMBS SECURE THE WEFTS INTO THE HAIR AND THE NATURAL HAIR BLENDS IN IMPERCEPTIBLY. THE RESULT IS INSTANT COLOUR THAT ENABLES YOU TO CHANGE THE ORDINARY INTO THE EXTRAORDINARY.

FREE SPIRIT

FOLLOWING THE INVENTION OF COLOUR WEFTS, I WENT ONE
STEP FURTHER TO DEVELOP THE IDEA FOR THIS SHOOT. I
BRAINSTORMED, PLANNED, AND THEN ON THE DAY, THREW ALL
MY ORIGINAL IDEAS OUT OF THE WINDOW.

THE CATALYST FOR THIS CHANGE OF DIRECTION WAS THE
INSPIRATION I RECEIVED FROM THE MODELS, THE VIBRANCY OF
THE MOOD IN NEW YORK AND MY DESIRE TO DO SOMETHING
DIFFERENT ONCE AGAIN.

AMERICAN MODELS, WHILE BEING TOTALLY PROFESSIONAL,
HAVE THAT SOMETHING EXTRA TO OFFER – THEY PARTICIPATE IN
THE SHOOT AND WORK WITH YOU.

TWO OF THE GIRLS I USED CUT THEIR HAIR THEMSELVES. THIS IS
A SIGN OF THE TIMES – GIRLS NOW KNOW WHAT LOOK THEY
WANT. THEY ARE SAYING THAT THEY DON'T WANT TO LOOK AS
THOUGH THEY HAVE JUST COME OUT OF THE SALON. THIS IS A
VERY IMPORTANT MESSAGE IN HAIR STATEMENT –
REMEMBER PUNK!

THE MODELS' HOME HAIRDRESSING WOULD ONCE HAVE BEEN
ANATHEMA TO ME, BUT THEIR CUTS ENCOURAGED ME TO GO
WITH THE UNSTRUCTURED LINE OF THEIR HAIR AND MOVE
FURTHER INTO UNCHARTED WATER TO CREATE A FREEDOM
WITHIN THESE STYLES.

THESE ARE THE MODELS WHO
HAD CUT THEIR OWN HAIR

COMMERCIAL IMAGES

'Less is more'

EVERY ONCE IN A WHILE, ARTISTRY HAS TO GO ON HOLD FOR ALL OF US AND WE HAVE TO PRODUCE COMMERICAL IMAGES. I FIND IT HARD TO RESTRAIN MYSELF AND NOT GET CARRIED AWAY.

TO CREATE SOMETHING THAT IS WEARABLE, AND AT THE SAME TIME HAS A TWIST, THAT LITTLE BIT OF EXTRA OOMPH THAT LIFTS IT FROM THE NORMAL, IS QUITE DIFFICULT.

THE POINT OF DIFFERENCE CAN BE THE HAIR, THE PROPS, THE MODEL, THE STYLE OF PHOTOGRAPHY OR MAKE-UP. I SOMETIMES FIND IT HARD TO HOLD BACK AND I HAVE TO REMIND MYSELF CONSTANTLY THAT, SOMETIMES, LESS IS MORE. THIS IS WHERE THE CHOICE OF MODEL BECOMES AN IMPORTANT ISSUE: IF THE HAIRSTYLE IS NOT THE STRONGEST PART OF THE IMAGE, THEN THE GIRL'S FACE BECOMES PARAMOUNT.

THIS IS AN EARLY ATTEMPT AT FREEHAND CUTTING IN THE FRINGE AREA. I LOVE THE AGGRESSIVE FEEL AND THE NON-TECHNICAL LOOK ABOUT IT, COUPLED WITH THE WISPS ON THE SIDE, WHICH COME TO LIFE WHEN BLOWN WITH THE WIND MACHINE.

A 60s-INSPIRED HAIRCUT. THIS IMAGE LATER BECAME ONE OF MY MOST SUCCESSFUL HAIR POSTERS.

96

EVEN VERY SHORT HAIR CAN BE DRESSED IN DIFFERENT WAYS TO MAXIMISE MODEL TIME.

MARK HAVRILIAK

MARK HAVRILIAK

INCORPORATING BODY SHAPE INTO THE PICTURE ADDS ANOTHER DIMENSION.

AN ORIGINAL TEXTURE WAS
CREATED USING CONDITIONER
AND CURL-FORMING PRODUCTS
BEFORE TWISTING AND DIFFUSER-
DRYING THEN DRESSING THE HAIR
INTO THIS CLASSIC STYLE.

WAX GIVES TEXTURE WHILE
CLOTHES STYLING AND MODEL
POSE GIVE THE MOOD.

AVANT
GARDE

'Pushing the boundaries'

THE ONE THING THAT KEEPS ME ALIVE AS A HAIRDRESSER IS TO TRY TO DO SOMETHING WITH HAIR THAT I HAVE NEVER SEEN BEFORE AND HAVE NO KNOWLEDGE OF HOW TO ACHIEVE.

WHY DO WE CREATE UNWEARABLE HAIRSTYLES? FOR ME THERE IS A VERY VALID REASON FOR THIS PHENOMENON. WE HAVE TO TRY TO PUSH THE BOUNDARIES AND STRETCH THE IMAGINATION INTO STATEMENTS WHICH CAN THEN BE DILUTED AND TURNED INTO SOMETHING COMMERCIAL. FASHION DESIGNERS USE THE SAME PHILOSOPHY ON THE CATWALKS, OFTEN CREATING UNWEARABLE CLOTHES JUST TO PUSH THE BOUNDARIES. ELEMENTS OF THESE BOLD STATEMENTS THEN FILTER THROUGH TO THE HIGH STREET.

THE PROCESS THAT I USE TO CREATE SUCH IDEAS IS VERY SIMPLE. I LOCK MYSELF IN MY STUDIO, WHERE I HAVE A LIBRARY OF REFERENCE BOOKS RANGING FROM PHOTOGRAPHY, FASHION AND ART TO CURRENT MAGAZINES. I USE THIS MATERIAL TO STIMULATE MY IMAGINATION. I DON'T ALWAYS STAY WITHIN THE REALMS OF HAIRDRESSING; I LOOK TO OTHER MEDIA AND MATERIALS. THE CREATIVE PROCESS CAN BE INSTANT OR IT CAN TAKE WEEKS.

THE FOLLOWING PHOTOGRAPHS STEM FROM IDEAS THAT I HAVE HAD OVER THE YEARS. IT IS EASY TO DO SOMETHING DIFFERENT, MUCH HARDER TO DO SOMETHING THAT IS BOTH DIFFERENT AND TASTEFUL. MY MESSAGE TO HAIRDRESSERS EVERYWHERE IS THIS: NEVER DISMISS THE EXTREME BUT TAKE INSPIRATION FROM IT AND EXPRESS IT IN YOUR OWN WORK.

ROBYN BEECHE

Showing at the Corcoran Gallery. Washington for Saks-Jandel.
Wednesday evening 12 September.
Tickets by invitation only from Saks-Jandel + the Corcoran Gallery of Art

Photo by Robyn Beeche. Hair by Trevor Sorbie
Makeup by Vivant Garta. Model Vivien Lynne.

© Zandra Rhodes (UK) 10 London England

Zandra Rhodes — ARTISTS Proof

107

Zandra Rhodes 80

Showing at Olympia's magnificent Pillar Hall
Tuesday 25 March at 2:30 p.m.

photo: Robyn Beeche
Wigstan: Richard Sharah
makeup by Pauline
model: Carole Hewison
gowethensty: meike mulligen
Zandra's own hair. + shoe hair: Norma of London
shoes:: Charles Jourdan
pistol: hair: Trevor Sorbie
hat: Graham Smith

Showing at Olympias Magnificent Pillar Hall

Tuesday evening 27th June

109

ADDING BALDNESS TO A WOMAN IS PROBABLY THE CRUELLEST THING YOU CAN DO. HERE, WITH THE USE OF BALD CAPS AND HAIRPIECES, I HAVE TRIED TO CREATE THE FEELING OF A SURREAL WARRIOR.

DAVID DARLING

I WAS INTO SCULPTURAL
SHAPES USING THE GIRLS' OWN
HAIR TO CREATE A THREE-
DIMENSIONAL LOOK. BELOW:
LAYING THE BLONDE PIECES ON
TOP OF THE GELLED HAIR
TRANSFORMED THE SIMPLE
INTO THE DRAMATIC.

DAVID DARLING

115

116

'The frizz'

IF YOU TAKE A TECHNIQUE THAT ALREADY EXISTS AND TURN IT AROUND, YOU WILL ACHIEVE A COMPLETELY DIFFERENT LOOK WHICH BEARS NO RELATION TO ITS ORIGINS.

A GOOD EXAMPLE OF THIS IS MY FRIZZ TECHNIQUE. IN THE STYLE ON pp. 124–125, I SET THE ENDS OF THE GIRLS' HAIR ON STRAIGHT HAIRPINS, CREATING AN INCREDIBLE FRIZZ EFFECT. IN THE STYLE ON p. 127, I REVERSED THE TECHNIQUE AND SET THE HAIR AT THE ROOTS USING THE SAME METHOD, LEAVING THE ENDS FREE. SEE THE DIFFERENCE – A COMPLETELY NEW SHAPE AND EFFECT.

WHAT A DIFFERENCE A DRYER MAKES.

126

MAGIC
MOMENTS

'If I can do it, so can you'

COMING FROM HUMBLE BEGINNINGS IN SCOTLAND, I NEVER
DREAMT THAT I WOULD ACHIEVE AS MUCH AS I HAVE. ALL I SET
OUT TO BE WAS A GOOD HAIRDRESSER, BUT I HAVE PROVED TO
MYSELF THAT IT'S NOT JUST ABOUT HOW CLEVER YOU ARE, IT'S
MORE ABOUT HOW DETERMINED YOU ARE.

I LOOK AT MY CAREER A BIT LIKE A LADDER. I SET MYSELF A
REACHABLE GOAL AND, WHEN I HAVE ACHIEVED IT, I SET
MYSELF ANOTHER GOAL. AFTER A WHILE YOU LOOK DOWN
FROM THAT LADDER AND REALISE THAT YOU HAVE CLIMBED A
FEW RUNGS, SO YOU MUST BE DOING SOMETHING RIGHT.

IF YOU HAVE A BURNING PASSION, COUPLED WITH
DETERMINATION, YOU CAN SURPRISE YOURSELF. IF YOU TRULY
BELIEVE IN YOURSELF, ANYTHING IS POSSIBLE... QUITE SIMPLY,
IF I CAN DO IT, SO CAN YOU!

ME AND MY HERO, VIDAL SASSOON, 1985.

DOES MY FACE NOT SAY IT ALL? BRITISH HAIRDRESSER OF THE YEAR 1985.

SHARING MY JOY – VIVIENNE MACKINDER, MY ARTISTIC DIRECTOR AT THE TIME, MY WIFE, KRIS, AND MY DAUGHTER, JADE.

CREATING POP GROUP TAKE THAT'S NEW LOOK, 1995.

I WAS HONOURED TO BE CHOSEN TO CREATE A HAIRSTYLE MADE OUT OF A ROLL OF KODAK FILM AND LAUNCHED BY SUPERMODEL CARLI BRUNI.

XAVIER WENGER PRESENTS ME WITH THE FELLOWSHIP FOR BRITISH HAIRDRESSING PATRON D'HONNEUR LIFETIME HAIRDRESSING AWARD 1993 – PREVIOUSLY AWARDED ONLY TO VIDAL SASSOON, ALEXANDRE DE PARIS AND RAYMOND, OBE.

'Showtime'

AWARDS

- Best Haircutter Worldwide 1997
- Most Newsworthy Male Hair Designer Worldwide (IBS Award) 1997
- Most Newsworthy Male Hair Designer Worldwide (IBS Award) 1996
- World Congress Hall of Fame, 1995
- Living Legend Award, New York, 1995
- Fellowship for British Hairdressing Patron d'Honneur Lifetime Hairdressing Award 1993
- Best Education Award (USA) 1993
- **British Hairdresser of the Year 1992**
- **British Hairdresser of the Year 1991**
- Avant-Garde Stylist of the Year 1991
- British Hairdressing Awards Hall of Fame 1991
- Foreign Stylist of the Year 1990 (voted by *Peluquerias* magazine)
- London Stylist of the Year 1989
- Avant-Garde Stylist of the Year 1989
- **British Hairdresser of the Year 1986**
- London Stylist of the Year 1986
- **British Hairdresser of the Year 1985**
- National Hairdresser of the Year 1985
- London Stylist of the Year 1985

ACKNOWLEDGEMENTS

With thanks to:

My parents, Edna and Robert Sorbie, without whom I would never have experienced the world of hair; my brother Michael for being the strength in the family and for always making himself available when I have needed him most; my wife, Kris, for supporting and believing in me; Grant Peet, my business partner, for his endurance and business skills, without which I wouldn't be where I am today; my daughter, Jade, for being honest with me; Vidal Sassoon, who revolutionised hairdressing as we know it today; the principal of the Richard Henry School of Hairdressing, Martin Gotlib, who saw something in those early days that I wasn't aware of; finally, photographer Mark Havriliak, whose constant creativity has kept me alive as a hairdresser over the last few years.

Photography

Robyn Beeche, pp. 106, 107*, 108*; Albert Chacon, pp. 118–119; David Darling, pp. 7, 115; Richard Dunkley, pp. 8, 9, 104; Mark Havriliak, pp. 41–43, 45–49, 51–53, 55–57, 59–61, 63–67, 79–83, 85–89, 98–99, 101; Alistair Hughes, pp. 11, 13, 19–29, 96, 112–113; Patrick Hunt, pp. 4–5; Trevor Leighton, p. 137; David Levine, pp. 15, 114; Bill Ling, pp. 33–35, 37–39, 93, 97, 111; Al McDonald, pp. 95, 110, 114, 117, 121; Grant Mudford, p. 109*; Peter Rosenbaum, Scope Features, courtesy of *OK Magazine*, p.135; John Swanell, p. 8; Taggart/Winterhalter, pp. 100, 116, 122, 124–127; Steve Woolard, p. 120; David Woolley, pp. 69–73, 75–77.

* As seen in *The Art of Zandra Rhodes*, published by Michael O'Mara Books Ltd, 1994.

THE END

HAIRDRESSING TRAINING BOARD/MACMILLAN SERIES

The Art of Hair Colouring
by David Adams & Jacki Wadeson

Patrick Cameron: Dressing Long Hair
by Patrick Cameron & Jacki Wadeson

Mahogany: Steps to Cutting, Colouring and Finishing Hair
by Martin Gannon & Richard Thompson

Start Hairdressing! – The Official Guide to Level 1
by Martin Green & Leo Palladino

Hairdressing – The Foundations: The Official Guide to Level 2
by Leo Palladino

Professional Hairdressing – The Official Guide to Level 3
by Martin Green, Lesley Kimber & Leo Palladino

Safety in the Salon: A Guide for Hairdressing and Beauty Professionals
by Elaine Almond

The World of Hair: A Scientific Companion
by John Gray

Hairdressing Training Board/Macmillan Series
Series Standing Order 0–333–69338–8

You can receive future titles in this series as they are published by placing a standing order. Please contact your bookseller or, in case of difficulty, write to us at the address below with your name and address, the title of the series and the ISBN quoted above.

Customer Services Department, Macmillan Distribution Ltd, Houndmills, Basingstoke, Hampshire RG21 6XS, England

Macmillan Press on the WWW
http://www.macpress.com

'We are all better hairdressers because of Trevor, the inspirer, motivator, entertainer, innovator - my favourite hairdresser.'

Charlie Miller.

'The World of Hair as we know it would not have been the same without the presence of Trevor.'

Scott Cole

'Our profession needs to have leaders who are creative and good technicians, and who work with aesthetic motivation and make hairstyles develop. Throughout my professional life the great hairdressers such as Trevor Sorbie have given me the courage to compete and have increased my enthusiasm for our profession. Trevor Sorbie is a good example to be followed and a person to be respected. Stay that way, Trevor, for many years.'

Lluis Llongueras

think, create,
you are a man of
the world of
. Thanks for
.'

'Trevor Sorbie has made our industry exciting, approachable and realistic. For me it means he is a legend. It has been a great honour to work with such an artist.'

Umberto Giannini

'Trevor has added professionalism to our industry that can never be matched. He's truly a living testament to the quote: "If your mind can conceive it, you can achieve it". Your passion and integrity are an inspiration to us all! Never stop!'

Your friend
Van Council

'I have known Trevor in excess of 25 years. Throughout this entire period he has continued to be the most incredible innovator of our craft. He has always been ahead of his time and an icon for thousands of other hairdressers. He has always remained humble and will always find time to talk to anyone in the industry. His appetite for our wonderful industry remains undiminished – long may it continue!'

Daniel Galvin

'Having been Trevor's business partner over the last decade, it has always surprised me how he gathers strength from year to year. He feels, senses and produces and is totally focused and into his art. He's not a bad partner either.'

Grant Peet
Managing Director, Trevor Sorbie International plc

'Raymond was delighted to see the high standards of hairdressing and technical ability going forward into the future, in the capable hands of an artist like Trevor Sorbie.'

Rosalie Raymond.
(Mrs Teasie - Weasie)

extraordinary years
a great
ty. It was always
whatever path he

'Never before have so many been given so much by one man for so long. His love affair with hair enables him to inspire hairdressers all over the world. All you wish yourself Trevor.'
Your old friend

Joshua Galvin.

Trevor So
for many t
included) b
calling him